EASY RENAISSANCE PIECES
FOR
CLASSICAL GUITAR

Compiled and edited by Jerry Willard

A superb collection of delightful music of the Renaissance,
arranged in standard notation and tablature.

T0066645

Cover art: *The Scale of Love* by Jean Antoine Watteau, oil on canvas (Getty Images)
Project Editor: David Bradley
Interior design and layout: Len Vogler

Speed • Pitch • Balance • Loop

To access companion recorded performance online, visit:
www.halleonard.com/mylibrary

Enter Code
6135-6234-0546-1481

ISBN 978-0-8256-3757-5

Visit Hal Leonard Online at
www.halleonard.com

World headquarters, contact:
Hal Leonard
7777 West Bluemound Road
Milwaukee, WI 53213
Email: info@halleonard.com

In Europe, contact:
Hal Leonard Europe Limited
1 Red Place
London, W1K 6PL
Email: info@halleonardeurope.com

In Australia, contact:
Hal Leonard Australia Pty. Ltd.
4 Lentara Court
Cheltenham, Victoria, 3192 Australia
Email: info@halleonard.com.au

Contents

Introduction

The *Renaissance* (which means "rebirth" or "revival") began around 1400 and ended in the early 1600s. The musicians and artists of the Renaissance looked back to classical models, spawning a new era of artistic growth. With the invention of the printing press, music became available to the public as never before.

There was a great flowering of sacred and instrumental music, including music for the lute. The lute was brought to Europe in the thirteenth century by the returning crusaders. It was originally played with a plectrum, usually a feather tip. Later, the plectrum was discarded in favor of plucking with the right-hand fingers, thereby creating more polyphonic capabilities. Of all the instruments of the Renaissance, the lute was without a doubt the most popular. The amount of music printed and hand-written for the lute is astounding.

The Renaissance Lute

The Renaissance lute had a single first string followed by five pairs of strings. Each single string or pairing of strings was called a *course*. An early Renaissance lute would have had six courses, but as the Renaissance moved forward, more strings were added. By the time it reaches the late-Renaissance composer Robert Johnson, the typical lute has nine courses.

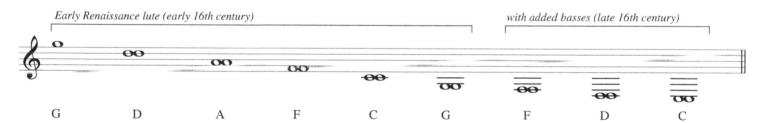

The Guitar

There is great similarity between present-day guitar tuning and the Renaissance lute, which makes the music in this book particularly adaptable to the guitar. The modern guitar, however, is tuned lower than the lute, so when this music is transcribed for the guitar, it is automatically lowered a minor third. It is very important to keep the string relationships the same to achieve the proper sound and playing conditions for each piece. The problem with this is that the bright (lute) key of G major becomes a lower, darker (guitar) key of E major. This is why, in this book, I recommend in most cases and have recorded the music with the use of a capo on the second fret. (In my opinion, the guitar sounds and reacts better with a capo at the second fret rather than the third fret.) In this way, the music maintains its lightness and charm and is also easier to play. It is indicated at the beginning of each piece whether it is recorded with a capo or not.

Rhythm

Much of the music in the Renaissance was based on dance forms and dance rhythms. Often the barlines and beaming are not indicative of what is actually happening in the music. This was especially prevalent in music that was in triple meter. A commonly used device in triple meter is called *hemiola*, meaning roughly the ratio 3:2. One of the most common uses of hemiola in this book is in the "Galliard", measures 8 and 9. Notice that the eighth note remains the same throughout; what changes is the accent:

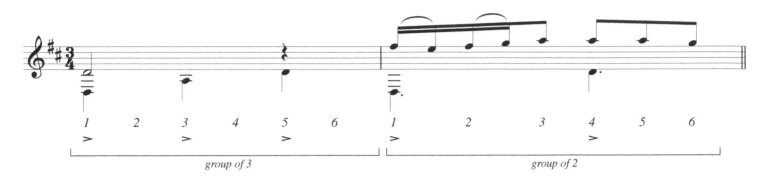

Another usage of hemiola is in the "Saltarello", measures 8 through 11. Here the duple (2) grouping is in the first two measures followed by the triple (3) grouping in the following two measures:

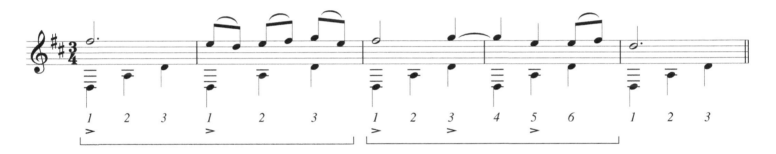

This rhythm was very important in Renaissance and Baroque dance and was used extensively in the music of these periods. Remember, it's only the accents that change. The quarter note or eighth note (depending on the piece) remains the same. Please listen to the included audio for further clarification.

In the Renaissance, the primary rhythmic note value was either the half note or whole note. In the present day, it's the quarter note. For example, it would have been common in the Renaissance to write "Mary Had A Little Lamb" like this:

Today, of course, it is written like this:

So just because the note values are larger, it doesn't necessarily mean that the tempo of the piece is slow. The included audio and metronome markings will help to make this clear.

Ornamentation

Much of the music of the Renaissance was improvised. A good performer would rarely play exactly what was written and would embellish it with various *divisions* and *graces*.

Divisions are embellishments that add extra notes and complex rhythms to a simple passage. Let's take a look at "Packington's Pound". The top staff is the melody as written in the first eight measures. The bottom staff shows how the author composed the divisions:

Another form of ornamentation is adding hammer-ons and pull-offs known as *graces*. Here is an example of this:

If there is a bass note, the first note of the grace is always played with the bass:

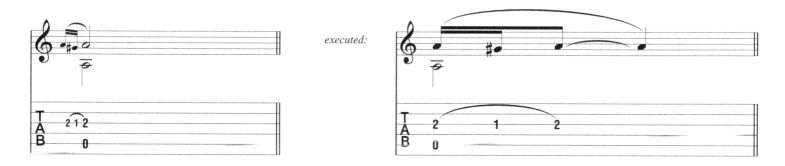

I have recorded "Peg-A-Ramsey" and "Tanz" first as it is written and then as a performer in the sixteenth century might have added ornaments. These are good examples of using both divisions and graces. For simplification, all of the pieces in this book can be played plain without any extra graces, even leaving out the graces that are written. For the more advanced and adventurous player, feel free to add extra graces and divisions.

Recording

In the process of recording these pieces, I decided to play the tempos that I felt the pieces should be played at, rather than too slowly for demonstration purposes. I also decided to use a capo to achieve the correct timbre and gesture that many of the compositions in this book require. There are many solutions to this depending on one's skill level, the quality of guitar, and musical aesthetic. The metronome markings are suggestions only and not meant to be a goal. A variety of tempos will work for many of the compositions in this book, so pick a comfortable tempo for your level of playing.

Jerry Willard
Stowe, Vermont, August 2010

A Jig

R. Askue (English, 16th century)

A Jig

Francis Cutting (c.1550–1595)

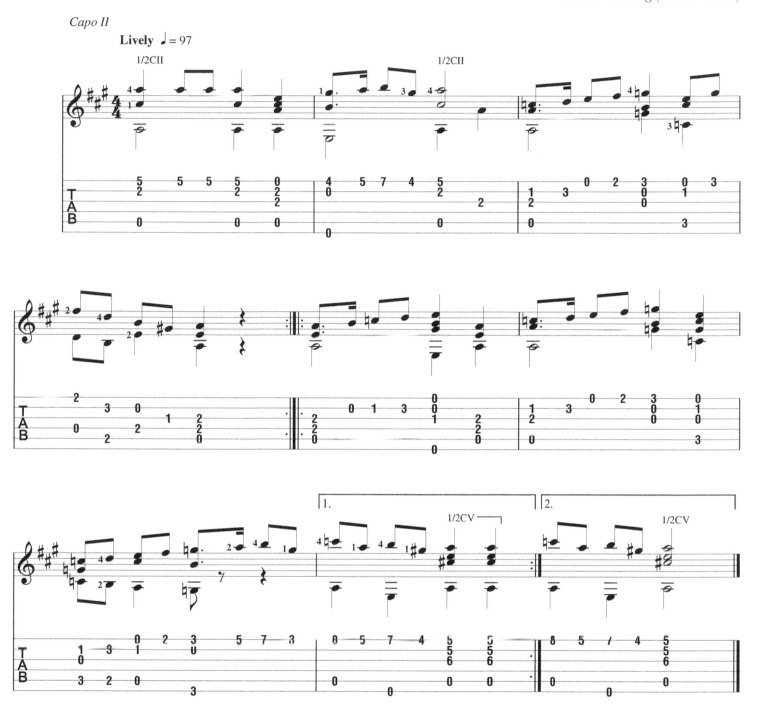

Almain

Robert Johnson (1583–1633)

Moderately ♩ = 118

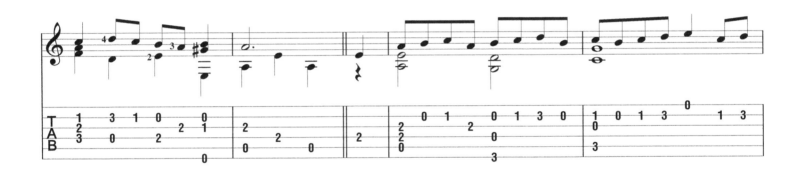

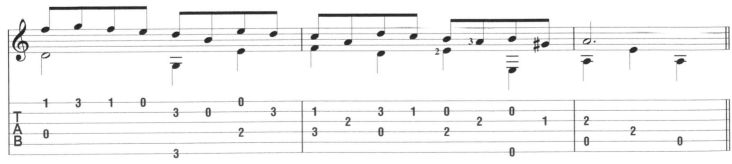

Ah Robyn, Gentle Robyn

William Cornyshe (1465–1523)

Almain

Richard Allison (c.1560–c.1610)

Capo II

Stately ♩ = 120

Balletto

Jean Baptiste Besard (1567–1617)

Basse Danse la Roque

Pierre Attaingnant (c.1495–c.1551)

Bianco Fiore

Cesare Negri (1536–1605)

Black Nag

(from *The Dancing Master*, 1657)

Anon. (English, 16th century)

⑥ = D
Capo II

Moderately ♩. = 57

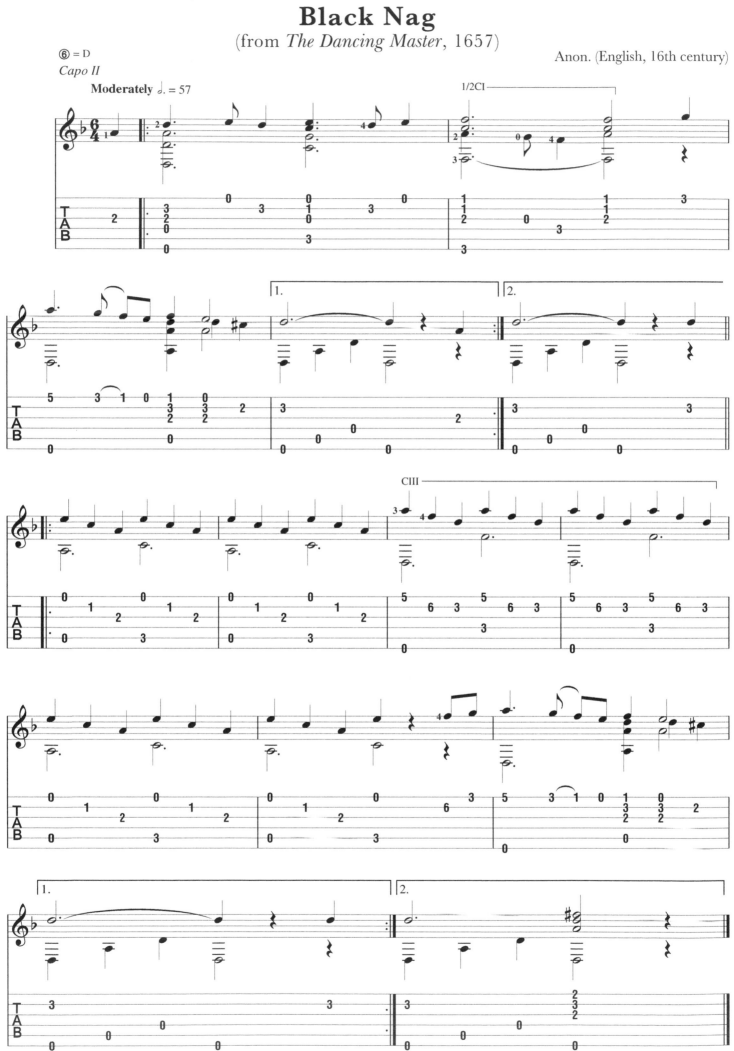

Bonny Sweet Boy

Anon. (English, 16th century)

Bonny Sweet Robin

Anon. (English, 16th century)

Capo II

Branle

Anon. (English, 16th century)

Capo II

Branle de la Cornemuse

Robert Ballard (c.1575–1649)

Branle de Village

Robert Ballard

Coventry Carol

Anon. (English, 15th century)

Capo II

Slowly ♩ = 84

Dove son quei fieri occhi?

Anon. (Italian, 16th century)

Fantasia

Anon. (Italian, 16th century)

Fortune My Foe

John Dowland (1563–1626)

Greensleeves

Anon. (English, 16th century)

Galliard

Anon. (Italian, 16th century)

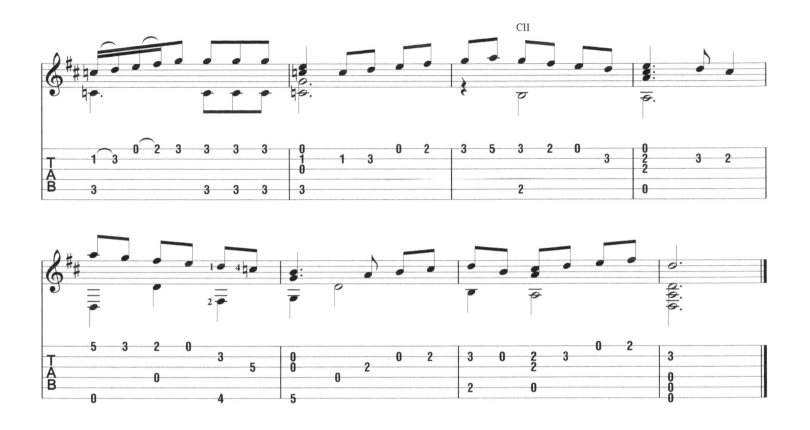

Go From My Window

Anon. (English, 16th century)

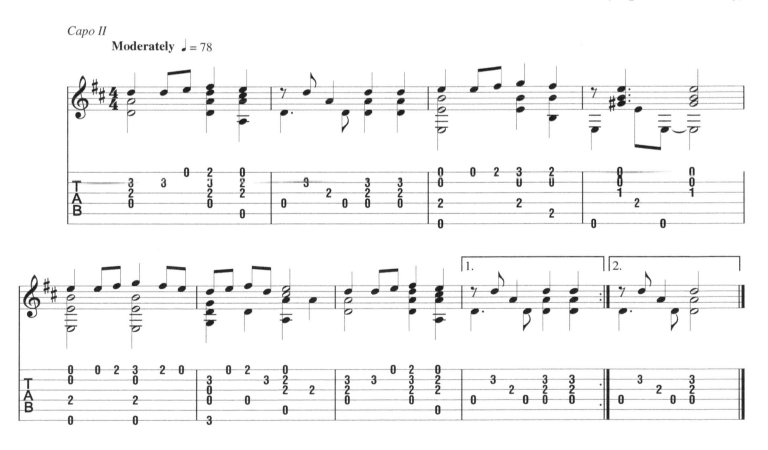

Ich Klag Den Tag

Hans Neusidler (c.1580–1563)

Kemp's Jig

Anon. (English, 16th century)

Les Bouffons

Jean d' Estrées (d.1576)

Loath To Depart

Anon. (English, 16th century)

Medieval Dance

Anon. (late 13th century)

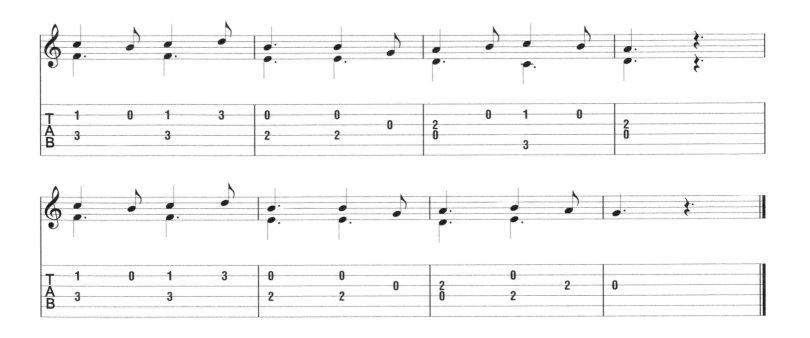

How Should I Your True Love Know?

(from *Hamlet*)

Anon. (English, 16th century)

Mille Regretz

Josquin des Prez (c.1450–1521)

Mr. Dowland's Midnight

John Dowland

Mrs. Nichols' Almain

John Dowland

Capo II

Mrs. Winter's Jump

John Dowland

My Lord Willoughby's Welcome Home

John Dowland

Capo II

Nonesuch

Anon. (English, 16th century)

Oh Mistress Mine

(from *Twelfth Night*)

Anon. (English, 16th century)

Capo II

Moderately ♩ = 60

Orlando Sleepeth

John Dowland

Packington's Pound

Anon. (English, 16th century)

Capo II

Moderately ♩ = 45

Pavana I

Luis Milan (c.1500–1561)

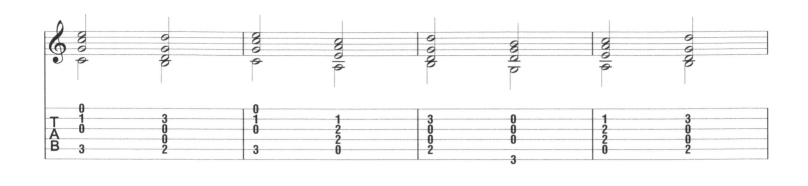

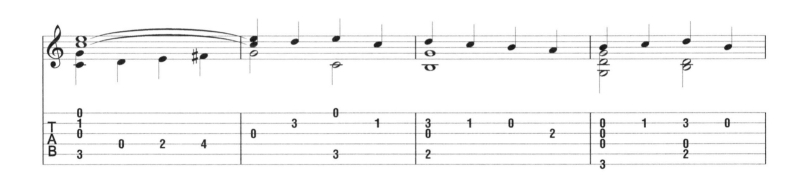

Pavana II

Luis Milan

Pastime With Good Company

Henry VIII (1491–1547)

Capo II

Moderately ♩ = 94

Peg-A-Ramsey

Anon. (English, 16th century)

Peg-A-Ramsey
(with ornamentation)

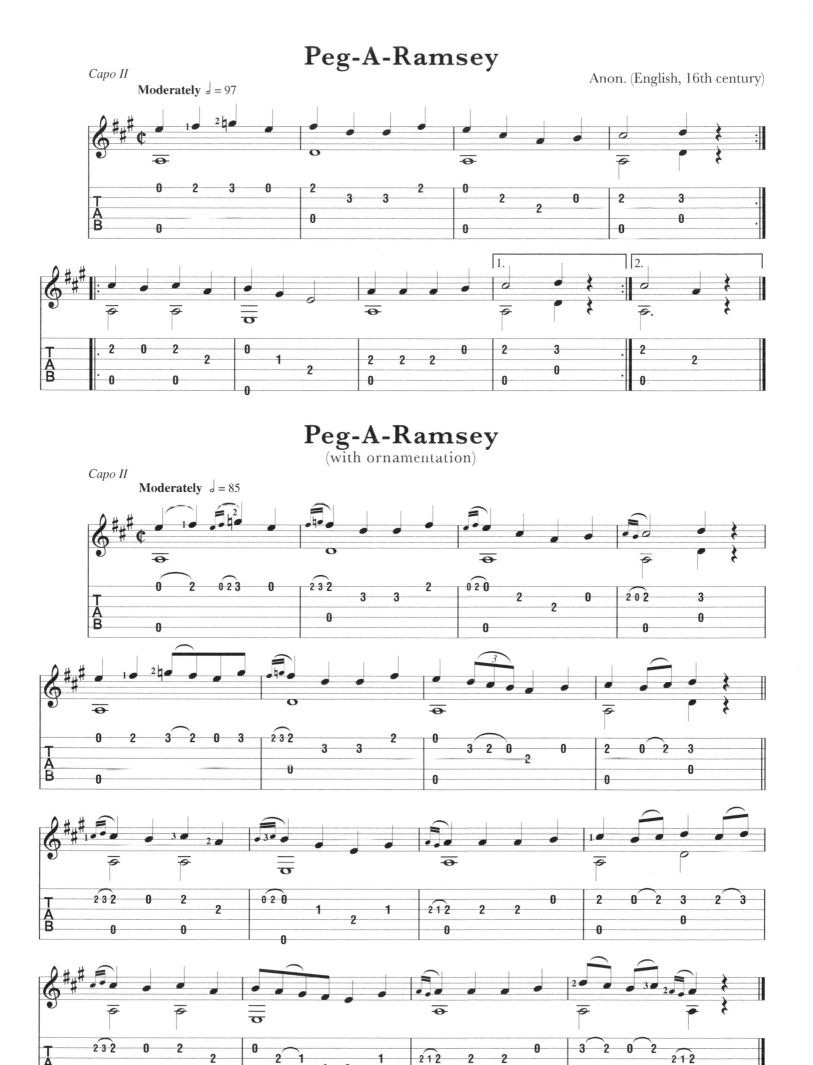

Pezzo Tedesco

Anon. (Italian, 16th century)

Capo II

Moderately ♩ = 63

Saltarello

Anon. (Italian, 16th century)

Scarborough Fair

Anon. (English, 16th century)

Se io m'accorgo be mio d'un altro amante

Anon. (Italian, 16th century)

Spagnoletta

Anon. (Italian, 16th century)

Tanz

Georg Leopold Fuhrmann (1574–1616)

Tanz

(with ornamentation)

⑥ = D

Moderately ♩. = 59

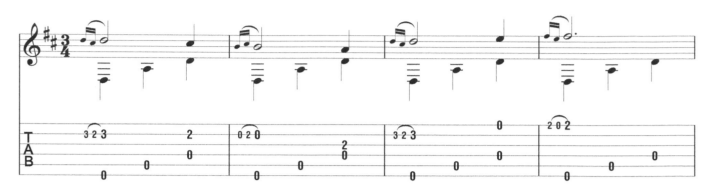
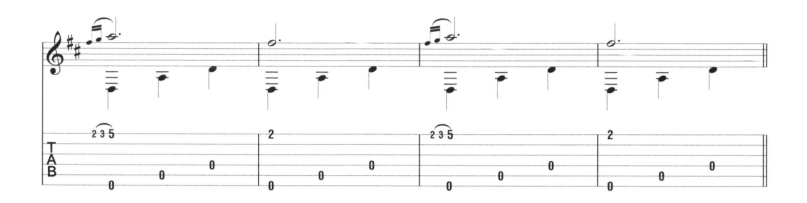
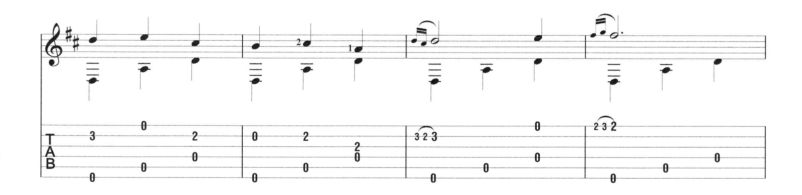

Tarleton's Resurrection

John Dowland

The Squirrel's Toy

Francis Cutting

There Were Three Ravens

Thomas Ravenscroft (c.1582–c.1635)

Capo II

Slowly ♩ = 84

Toy

Francis Cutting

Toy
(from *Jane Pickering's Lute Book*)

Anon. (English, 16th century)

Capo II

Moderately ♩. = 63

Toy
(from *Jane Pickering's Lute Book*)

Anon. (English, 16th century)

Capo II

Lively ♩ = 100

Vaghe belleze et bionde treccie d'oro vedi che per ti moro

Anon. (Italian, 16th century)

Volte

Anon. (English, 16th century)

Volte

Michael Praetorius (1571–1621)

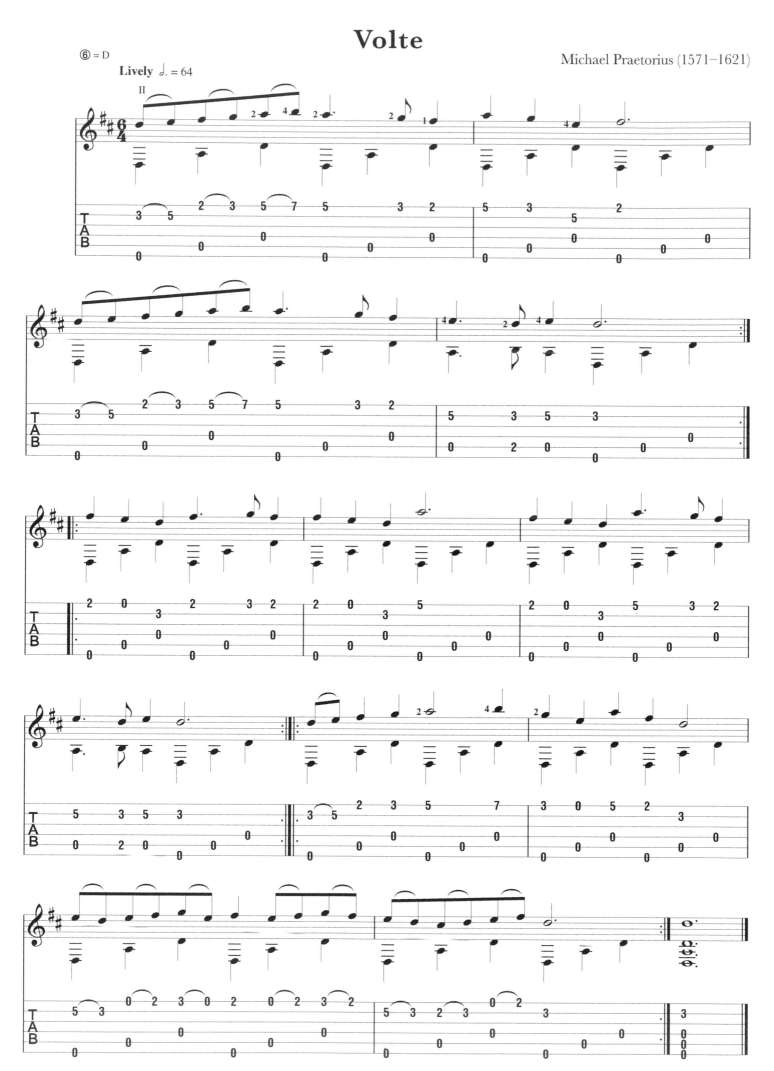

What If A Day Or A Month Or A Year

Anon. (English, 16th century)

When That I Was And A Little Tiny Boy

(from *Twelfth Night*)

Anon. (English, 16th century)

Where The Bee Sucks

(from *The Tempest*)

Robert Johnson

Capo II

Moderately ♩ = 112

Willow, Willow

(from *Othello*)

Anon. (English, 16th century)

Capo II

Slowly ♩ = 66

Wilson's Wilde

Capo II

Anon. (English, 16th century)

Woodycock

(from *The English Dancing Master*, 1651)

Anon. (English, 16th century)